Contents

Introduction

Pocket Playground Ga
World Volume 1 focus_ _. . . .... ._.. .._., and
includes games from China, Korea, Kenya, India
and Russia (Russia spans Asia and Europe).
Although we have tried to include as many
countries as possible in this volume, we have
not been able to include every country, but
there will be more booklets in the series.

The traditions and traits of different cultures
are often reflected through the games that
children play. Although many childhood
games are very similar, a different culture will
often offer an alternative twist which adds to
the fun!

The games in these booklets not only
encourage energetic exercise, promote
valuable social skills and positive relations
between the children themselves, they may
also encourage children to find out more about
the lives of children from other countries,
and as schools often have a broad cultural
mix themselves, this is an ideal opportunity
to engage children in enjoyable activities
together. Children with links to these countries
often feel very proud that their games are
included and you could encourage these
children to ask their parents, grandparents and
other relatives to teach them more games.

The games are set out in a clear, accessible
style with easy-to-follow instructions. Where
possible we have included key words, rhymes
or chants in the original country's language
alongside the English to encourage children to
try a different language if they feel like it.

For those children with origins in the country concerned, they can feel a special pride in helping to teach the game to others.

We hope the games in this book will spark off children's cultural interest and curiosity about these countries and encourage them to see how games link us all together as "one world" through a universal language of fun.

Bangladesh
Ayanga-ayanga (The Tiger and the Goats)

Background/history: Traditional folk games in Bangladesh were chiefly played in rural areas and passed along from one generation to another. Such games are played for physical exercise and entertainment, at times in a competitive environment.

Number of players: 4-8

You will need: A piece of chalk to draw a large circle on the ground.

How to play:

A large circle is drawn on the ground. One player plays the role of the tiger and remains outside the circle, while the other players play goats and stay inside it.

The "Tiger" pretends to be crying and enters into a conversation with the goats (singing rather than talking). The conversation could go something like this:

Tiger (pretending to cry): **Weep, weep!**

Goats (in chorus): **Why are you crying, crying?**

Tiger: **I lost my cow**

Goats: **What colour is your cow?**

Tiger: **It was a red cow**

Goats: **Does it have horns?**

Tiger: **Yes**

Goats: **Please sing us a song!**

The tiger then starts dancing and "singing" (more a dramatic wailing!):

"Who took my cow?

Who took my cow?
Come here whoever took my cow!
Please let me have my cow back!"

The tiger is trying to distract the goats with his singing. Suddenly the tiger stops and jumps forward to drag one of the goat players outside the circle. The other goats try to hold him back so that the tiger cannot take the goat away.

The goats taken out of the circle by the tiger belong to the tiger's side. The last player in the circle becomes the tiger in the next round.

Botswana
Deweke

Background/history: A traditional game to encourage jumping and foot skills.
Number of players: 2 or more.
What you need: A number of small plastic beakers or cups (at least 4 per player) and a large, shallow container, such as a plastic bowl. (Cans were used traditionally, but we recommend plastic cups or similar safe containers!)

How to play:

Place the larger container in the middle of the area you wish to play the game in – not too far away – this is the target.

Players take turns to try and get the small cans or cups into the target using only their feet – by placing one of their plastic cups or beakers between their feet and jumping, trying to drop it into the target. If successful they have another go.

The winner is the player who gets the most cups or beakers into the target container.

China
Catch The Dragon's Tail

Background/history: In China the dragon is a symbol of power, strength, and good luck and this traditional Chinese game is great fun for the playground. This game fits in well with Chinese New Year celebrations when there are street festivals with dancing dragons.

Number of players: At least 8 – but the more the merrier.

What you need: Possibly a handkerchief depending on the version played.

How to play:

The children all form a line with their hands on the shoulders of the child in front. The first in line is the dragon's head, the last in line is the dragon's tail.

The dragon's head then tries to catch the tail by manoeuvring the line around so that he can tag the last player. All the players in the middle do their best, by keeping their arms stiff, to hinder the dragon's head. The line is not allowed to break.

When the head catches the tail, the tail player takes the front position and becomes the new dragon's head. All the other players move back one position.

A great variation:

A line of children, as above, hold on to each other's shoulders.

One child is chosen to be the "catcher" and is not in the dragon line.

A scarf is tucked into the waistband of the last

child at the tail of the dragon. The catcher, who is free, faces the dragon's head (i.e. the first child in the line at the front of the dragon). The catcher tries to get to the tail of the dragon to capture the scarf. By pretending to go one way, then the other, the catcher, facing the dragon's head, tries to confuse the dragon in order to get to the end of the tail to grab the scarf.

Note:

I have played this game a lot in the playground and the children love it! You could even fashion a lovely dragon's head and tail when it's Chinese New Year.

China
Four Seasons

Background/history: This traditional Chinese game is used to teach the names and order of the four seasons, so is particularly useful for younger players.
Number of players: 8 or more.
What you need: Nothing.

How to play:

The players are divided into four groups to represent the four seasons and named Spring, Summer, Autumn and Winter.

The groups sit down.

The leader says:

"I am Spring and I am leaving."

The group representing Summer stands up and the players say:

"I am Summer and I am coming."

The leader says:

"I am summer and I am leaving."

Summer group sit down and Autumn group stand and say:

"I am Autumn and I am coming."

The game continues in this way with the seasons being presented in the correct order.

Once the children are familiar with which season follows which, the leader chooses seasons in a random order. The players have to be particularly vigilant to know when to stand and say their chant.

Note:

With older children, the groups can be muddled up so that each groups contain players from all four seasons. The players have to be even more vigilant to know when to stand and say their chant.

China
Shan-Dian-Didi

Background/history: A Chinese tag game in which children practise being focused. "Shan-Dian" means lightning and "Didi" normally means young boy, but in this game it is just a sound.
Number of players: 8 or more.
What you need: Nothing.

How to play:

A player is chosen to be the "ghost". The remaining players spread out in the available space.

When the ghost approaches a player, the player must clap their hands and say, **"Shan-Dian-Didi"**, before the ghost tags them. If they manage this, they are only frozen and if tagged can be rescued when being touched by another player.

Any player who is tagged by the ghost before clapping and saying, **"Shan-Dian-Didi"**, becomes the new ghost.

Egypt
The Handkerchief Game

Background/history: This is a traditional Egyptian game that is played widely across the country.

Number of players: 2 equal sized teams of 5 or more players and one leader.

You will need: Chalk to create the playing space – which is two parallel lines 20m apart – and to draw the leader's small circle in the centre – between the two lines – and a handkerchief. For safety make sure the area is free of debris.

How to play:

The leader stands holding up a handkerchief in a circle drawn in the centre of the playing area.

Players in each team are numbered one to five (above if there are more than five players).

The game begins by the leader holding up the handkerchief with arm extended calling a number from one to five (above if there are more than five players).

The two players from each team with this number quickly run into the circle to try to grab the handkerchief from the leader. The player who succeeds in grabbing the handkerchief tries to run back to his or her line without being tagged by their opposite number.

The player wins a point for their team if this task is completed successfully. If the player is tagged then the point goes to the opposite team.

India
Denga Pani (Land and Water)

Background/history: This traditional tag game is from the State of Bihar in the North-Eastern part of the Country.

Number of players: 6 or more.

What you need: The game is best played on higher and lower ground, but this is not essential. If the ground is flat, you will need to designate two different areas for "land" and "water".

How to play:

One player is chosen to be the "Magar" (crocodile) and occupy the **"Pani"** (water) – this will be the lower ground.

The remaining players occupy the **"Denga"** (land) – this will be the higher ground.

The players of the Denga, venture into the Pani and taunt the Magar with their song:

Hum tumhare pani me, pakado.
(I am in your area, catch me if you can.)

The Magar chases the players and tries to touch them. Anyone who is tagged is out. The game continues until the Magar has tagged all the players or is out of breath.

A new Magar is chosen and the game continues.

India
Satoliya (Seven Stones)

Background/history: This traditional game from Andhra Pradesh is also known as *Pithoo Phod* in some areas. It is fun and easy to set up and play.
Number of players: 2 or more.
What you need: Seven plastic building bricks (traditionally played with small flat stones) in ever decreasing sizes. Bean-bags or "balls" made from rolled material scraps.

How to play:

The stones are built into a tower, with the largest at the bottom, leading to the smallest at the top.

Players stand behind a designated line, dependent on age and throwing ability.

They take turns to throw their bean-bags or balls to try and knock down the tower.

Indonesia
Semut, Orang, Gajah (Ant, Person, Elephant)

Background/history: The large Indonesian island of Sumatra is home to the Sumatran elephant, which has made its way into this game. Similar to the American *Rock, Paper, Scissors*, children play *Semut, Orang, Gajah* to determine who goes first in another game or simply for fun. The word "orangutan" comes from the Indonesian words "orang," meaning "person," and "hutan," meaning "forest". Orangutans are native to Indonesia.
Number of players: 2 or more.
What you need: Nothing.

How to play:

Two players face each other and hold out a fist in front of them.

On the count of three, each makes one of the following three hand signs:

Semut (pronounced **suh-MOOT**), means ant: pointing with the little finger.

Orang (**orr-AHNG**), means person: pointing with the index finger.

Gajah (**gha-jah**), means elephant: pointing with the thumb.

How to score:

Semut vs orang, orang wins (a person can step on an ant).

Semut vs gajah, semut wins (an ant can crawl in an elephant's ear and bite or tickle it).

Gajah vs orang, gajah wins (an elephant can stomp on a person).

If players make the same signs, they go again.

Two out of three wins.

Israel
Blind Cow

Background/history: There are plenty of different versions of this blindfold game from different countries, several have a different twist.

Number of players: Any number.

What you need: Blindfolds for all who are participating apart from the instructor.

How to play:

One player is chosen to be the instructor. The others are blindfolded and stand as separate organised groups in front of the instructor. They must know which group they are standing with before they put their blindfolds on.

Play starts by the instructor calling out drill commands or marching instructions such as **"march forward"**, **"march with straight legs in a line to the right"**, **"march on the spot"** that must be carried out straight away and until the instructor blows a whistle or rings a cow bell and says, **"Stop"**.

The players must stop where they are and the group judged to have stayed together in the best formation is the winner.

Points for each win may be given and the team that accumulates the greatest number of points at the end of play is the overall winner.

Japan
Hana, Hana, Hana, Kuchi

Background/history: *Hana, hana, hana, kuchi* simply means *nose, nose, nose, mouth*. A little similar to *Follow The Leader* or *Simon Says*, this game will teach children simple Japanese words as well as concentration and coordination.

You will need: Traditionally played with flour and water, but this may not be suitable for school playgrounds where it could get rather messy. Perhaps the children put their hands on their cheeks instead of daubing cheeks with flour and water...

Number of players: 8 or more.

How to play:

The players sit in a circle and imitate the leader, who taps his or her nose three times and mouth once, while saying **"hana, hana, hana, kuchi"**, meaning, **"nose, nose, nose, mouth"**.

The leader continues to repeat the phrase but may touch any features in any order, regardless of the words being said. The players must do what the leader says and not what the leader does. A player failing to do this must become the leader or allow his or her cheek to be daubed with flour and water (or put their hands on their cheeks for a less messy game).

The names of the features are:

me (eye)

mimi (ear)

hana (nose)

kuchi (mouth)

Kazakhstan
Bayga (Horse Races)

Background/history: This is a racing game. Kazakhstan is thought to be the land where man first tamed the wild horse, and a place where horses are still prized.
Number of players: 4-8 (played in pairs).
What you need: A handkerchief or piece of cloth.

How to play:

Best played outside on grass with enough space to run. The handkerchief or piece of cloth is loosely tied up at a high (not too high) point near the finishing line or someone could be designated to stand at the finish line and loosely hold the cloth between forefinger and thumb.

Each pair decides who is the "horse" and who is the "rider". The horse stands in front of the rider and puts his or her arms down behind them. The rider takes hold of the horse's hands and, running together like this, they race the other pairs to the finish line. The players can only speak to one another as horses or riders – they can whinny or neigh like a horse, or the rider can say "giddy-up".

The handkerchief should be tied up (or held up) high enough so that the horse and rider pairs have to work together in order to reach it. However, the horse can hoist up the rider, so that the riders can reach up and pull down the handkerchief, but the rider cannot hoist up the horse. The first pair to grab the handkerchief wins.

Kenya
Nyama-nyama-nyama

Background/History: "Nyama" literally means "meat" in Swahili. This game is still played across East Africa and is popular amongst children of all ages.
Number of players: 4-12.
You will need: A list of animals, birds, fish and plants.

How to play:

One player is chosen as a leader.

The rest of the players sit in a circle around the leader who stands in the middle of the circle reading slowly from the list (unless they are confident to come up with their own list).

Each time the leader says the name of an animal that can be eaten, anyone in the group can jump up and shout **"Nyama"**. The first person who jumps up to shout **"Nyama"** is the winner and becomes the leader.

You could do a vegetarian version with the names of plants if you prefer.

Korea
Sam Pal Sun

Background/History: *Sam Pal Sun* is a tag game from Korea and is the name of the border between North and South Korea. Sam Pal Sun is a team game that requires speed and agility.

Number of players: 10 in total with 5 in each team or any number of players that have equal teams.

You will need: A flag and something to mark off a borderline.

How to play:

The two teams, A and B, line up facing one another across a "border" made from laying markers in a straight line on the ground. The teams take turns to be the defenders. Team A starts as the defenders and places a flag on the ground behind their team members. Each team member has a "territory" to defend and must stay in their territory.

Team B crosses the border and tries to capture the flag without being tagged. If they are tagged, they must "freeze", until released by being re-tagged by another member of team B. If all the team B players are tagged then the game stops. All Team B players return to their territory and the game restarts until they capture the flag.

Once team B capture the flag, they become the defenders and the flag is placed on the ground behind their team members. Team A then try to capture the flag in the same way.

Korea
Dan Chhae Jul Normgi

Background/history: A traditional game played for many centuries that is still popular today.
Number of players: 5 or more.
What you need: A long skipping rope.

How to play:

Two players take either end of the skipping rope and keep turning it. The remaining players stand in a line and one at a time attempt to jump over the rope.

If the skipper times it right, they will be able to stop the rope with their legs, this means they are the winner and they swap places with one of the rope turners.

Alternatively, if the rope turners "catch" the skipper's legs with the rope, the skipper is out.

The game continues in this way until only one skipper is left and they are the winner.

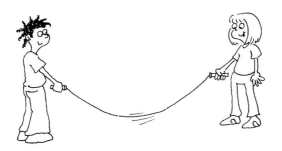

Lesotho
Mokou

Background/history: *Mokou* (pronounced mo-koo) is traditionally played with a selection of flattish stones that children find on the ground around their homes. For safety sake we recommend that you use wooden or plastic bricks.

Number of players: 2 teams of 5.

What you need: A quantity of wooden or plastic bricks. A softball.

How to play:

The players are divided into two teams of five, one team are the "builders" and the other are the "throwers". A player from the builders' team is chosen to begin the building. They pile bricks or stones on top of each other to form a tower. The other builders try to guard this player from the throwers. (They must stand at least a metre away from the builder). The throwers also have to stand more than a metre out and they try to hit the main builder with the soft ball. They can pass the ball amongst themselves to get a better shot. When the main builder is hit, that child is out and one of the "guarding builders" takes their place.

The game continues until all builders are out. The number of stones/bricks in their tower is counted. If the tower collapses during play, they must start building again. The team with the most number of stones/bricks in their tower wins.

The players can swap roles and the builders become throwers and vice versa.

Philippines
Tinikling

Background/history: One of the oldest traditional Filipino dances, the Tinikling dance, or bamboo dance, is performed using long bamboo poles. Originating on the island of Leyte in the central Philippines, the Tinikling dance is said to take its name from the tikling bird. The movements of the dance are meant to imitate the bird as it steps through its marshy habitat.

Number of players: At least 3.

You will need: Originally played with bamboo poles, you could use hollow plastic poles – you can now buy Tinikling cords or hollow Tinikling poles or sticks online easily. You may wish to view a sample of the dances online before starting this game.

How to play:

A wonderful take on skipping and dance, Tinikling can be likened to jump rope, but instead of a spinning rope, two bamboo poles are used. The two poles are held by two kneeling people, one pole in each hand. They tap the poles on the floor, then raise them slightly, then tap the poles together lengthways rhythmically, sometimes to music. The pole holders tap and slide the poles on the ground and against each other in co-ordination with dancers who step over and in between the poles in time. The person(s) in the middle hop over and outside the poles while the poles are apart. As the skippers gather confidence, the moving and tapping of the sticks together can become faster and harder.

Skilled Tiniklers do certain moves in a certain order – jumping with both feet inside the poles, one foot in and one foot outside and so on – there are plenty of "How to" videos online (Tip – For a video of the basic steps visit YouTube).

WARNING:

Be careful, this game can hurt ankles if the sticks are used aggressively or if the wrong equipment is used!

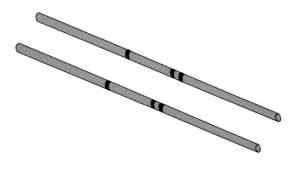

Russia
Edible - Inedible

Background/history: During the Soviet era, children would play in the yard outside their apartment building or house. There was a wonderful culture of "yard games" that were developmental, educational, as well as being fun!

Number of players: Variable numbers of children.

You will need: A ball.

How to play:

All players sit or stand in a row. One player is the lead player who stands in front facing the row and who throws a ball to one of the participants and at the same time calls out the name of an object. If the object is edible, the player catches the ball. If not, he bounces it away.

The leader tries to confuse the player, for example, by saying **"apple - melon - carrot - potato"** in a row, and then suddenly saying **"iron".**

If a player makes a mistake and "eats" the inedible object, he then becomes the new leader. The faster the leader throws the ball and calls out the object, the more exciting and fun the game becomes.

This game develops the ability to listen carefully and respond quickly.

Somalia
Gris or Grille

Background/history: This game is similar to *Jacks* that was played in Ancient Rome, Greece and Egypt.
Number of Players: 2 to about 6.
What you need: 2 shallow holes in the ground not too far apart and 13 stones or pebbles (plastic counters or small balls) each.

How to play:

Each player starts with 13 small pebbles, 12 of which are dropped into one of the shallow holes. They then toss the 13th or "throw" stone up into the air, and while it's in the air, picking up just one of the "grab" stones before catching the throw stone. The first grab stone is then dropped into the second hole. This is repeated with the throw stone until all grab pebbles have been transferred from the first to the second hole.

An alternative game is to have a single hollow filled with pebbles. Each player, in turn, tosses a throw pebble and scoops up as many grab pebbles as they can before catching the throw pebble. This continues until all the pebbles have been collected from the hollow. Each player then counts how many pebbles they have scooped and the one with the most is the winner.

Warning:

This game is not suitable for young children and we recommend playing with safe counters or small balls, instead of stones, and chalking a "hole" on the ground instead of digging.

South Africa
Mbube, Mbube

Background/history: "Mbube" (mboo-bay) is a Zulu word for lion. An impala is a Southern African antelope. In this game, the "lion" tries to capture the impala "buck".
Number of players: 12 or more.
What you need: 2 blindfolds.

How to play:

The players stand in a circle. One player is chosen to be the mbube (lion) and another player is chosen to be the impala buck.

The lion and buck wear blindfolds and stand on opposite sides of the circle. The lion tries to locate and capture the buck within the circle. The remaining players chant **"mbube, mbube" ("lion, lion")**.

They chant slowly when the lion and buck are on opposite sides of the circle, but the chanting gets faster and faster as the lion gets nearer the buck.

If the buck moves away from the lion, the chanting becomes slower again.

Allow a set time for the lion to capture the buck, then change the players.

Thailand
Kratai Kha Diew (One Legged Rabbit)

Background/history: *Kratai Kha Diew* is a version of tag from Thailand. There seem to be many different ways you can play this game depending on the region of Thailand you are in. The history is not clear but it is thought that is has evolved from a simple game of *Catch* or *Khee Naed*. Some of the rules and features of the game also resemble a traditional game called *Teoi*, so it is possible the game is a hybrid of the two.

Number of players: Two teams of equal numbers. Three or more in each team, but no more than 6 per team.

You will need: Bibs or cloths for the rabbits and cones or something to set the boundaries with. You could even use coloured chalk to mark the area out with.

How to play:

Mark an area in chalk on the playground or with cones if inside. The size and shape of the area will depend on the number of players in each team. For small teams, a large square can be drawn measuring approximately 7 x 7 metres. Bigger teams will need a rectangle measuring approximately 10 x 7 metres.

One team is chosen to be the "rabbits" who wear a bib or tabard. Rabbits must stay outside the marked area. The non-rabbit players must remain inside the marked area.

The rabbits take turns to enter the marked area – while hopping on one leg, if their other leg touches the ground they are out. The rabbits have to try to tag as many of the other players inside the area that they can. Any tagged players then become rabbits and leave the area to wait outside until it is their turn to go in again. The rabbit who entered the area becomes a normal player and stays inside the marked area.

If a player inside the boundary steps outside it, he or she is out, if a rabbit puts down his or her other foot then he or she is out. The game ends when one team or the other runs out of players and the winning team is the one that is left (or the one with the most players at the end if a timed game).

Vietnam
Meo Duoi Chuot (Cat Catches Mouse)

Background/history: *Meo Duoi Chuot* (sometimes known as *Meo Duoi Chait*), is, as it sounds, a Vietnamese game of *Cat and Mouse*.
Number of players: 6-12.
You will need: Nothing.

How to play:

One child is chosen to be the "mouse" and one is chosen to be the "cat".

All the other players stand in a circle holding hands. The children in a circle raise their hands to form arches or "holes" for the cat and mouse to run in and out of.

The children sing a song of their choice and when the song is over, the mouse runs in and out through the holes in an attempt to escape the cat. The cat must run after the mouse, following the same route. The cat wins the game when it catches the mouse. The mouse becomes the cat and a new mouse is chosen.

The challenge for the cat is that it has to follow exactly the same route that the mouse has taken, if he or she goes through a wrong hole, then the mouse becomes the cat and a new mouse is chosen.